Letters to my baby boy

18 years of birthday letters to my beloved son, to cherish for a lifetime.

To:
_____

With love from:
_____

Sofie K. Alexander

You were born on _____

Newborn Photo

love

Happy
Birthday

"No one prepared me for just how much love I would have for you, my son."

Date: _____

How we celebrated your 1st birthday:

What you're like at 1:

Best memories from this year:

My wishes for you:

My advice for you:

More thoughts...

Happy
Birthday

"Let me love you a little more before you're not little anymore."

Date:

How we celebrated your 2nd birthday:

What you're like at 2:

Best memories from this year:

My wishes for you:

My advice for you:

More thoughts...

Happy
Birthday

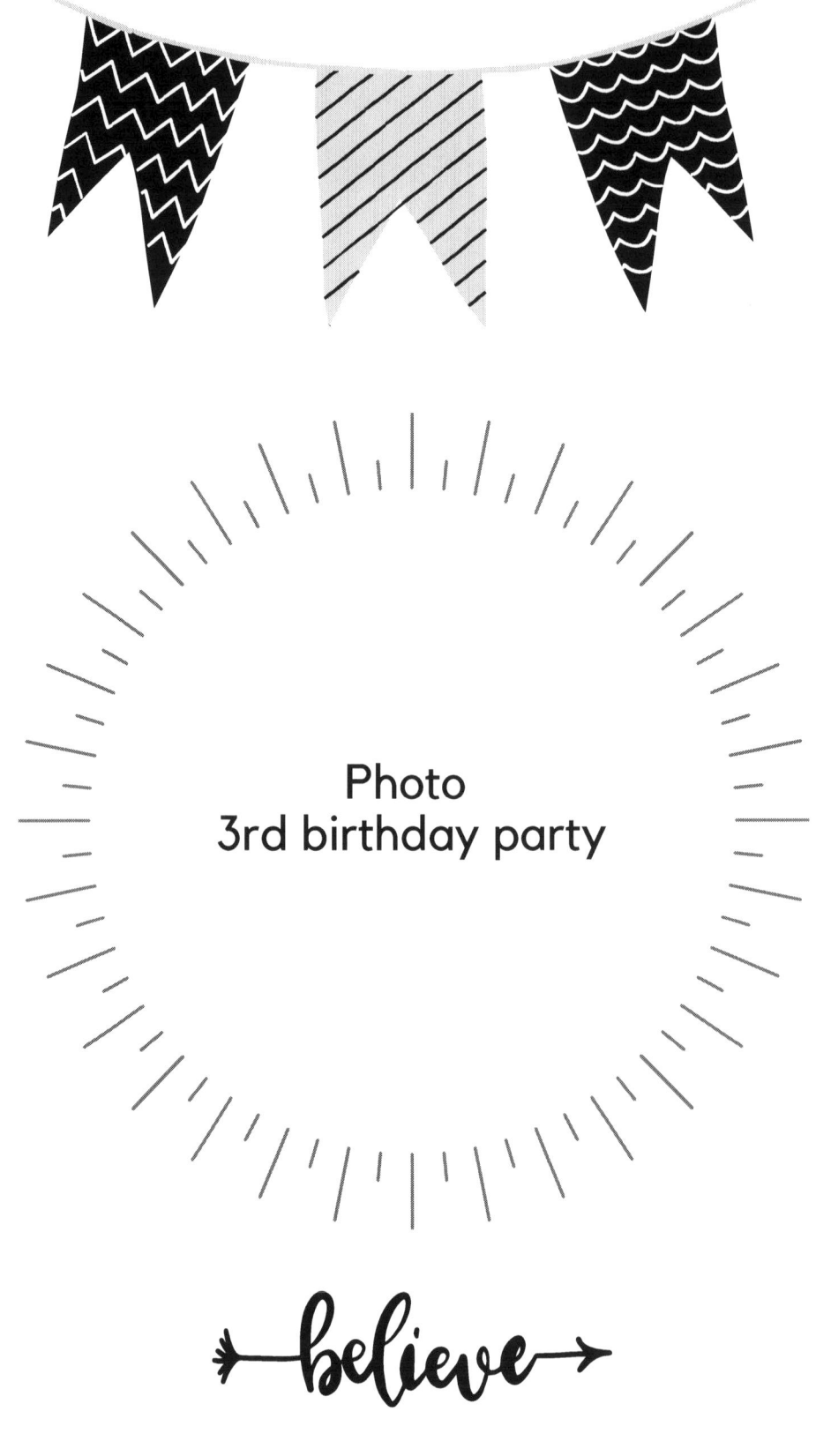

"My baby boy, you are my heart!"

Date: _____

How we celebrated your 3rd birthday:

What you're like at 3:

Best memories from this year:

My wishes for you:

My advice for you:

More thoughts...

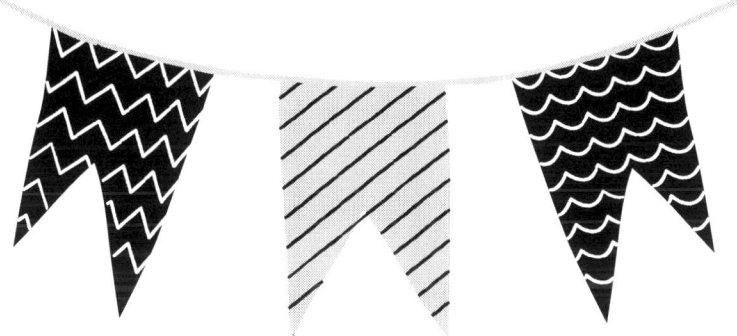

Happy
Birthday

"Happiness is...seeing my son growing up."

Date:

How we celebrated your 4th birthday:

What you're like at 4:

Best memories from this year:

My wishes for you:

My advice for you:

More thoughts...

Happy
Birthday

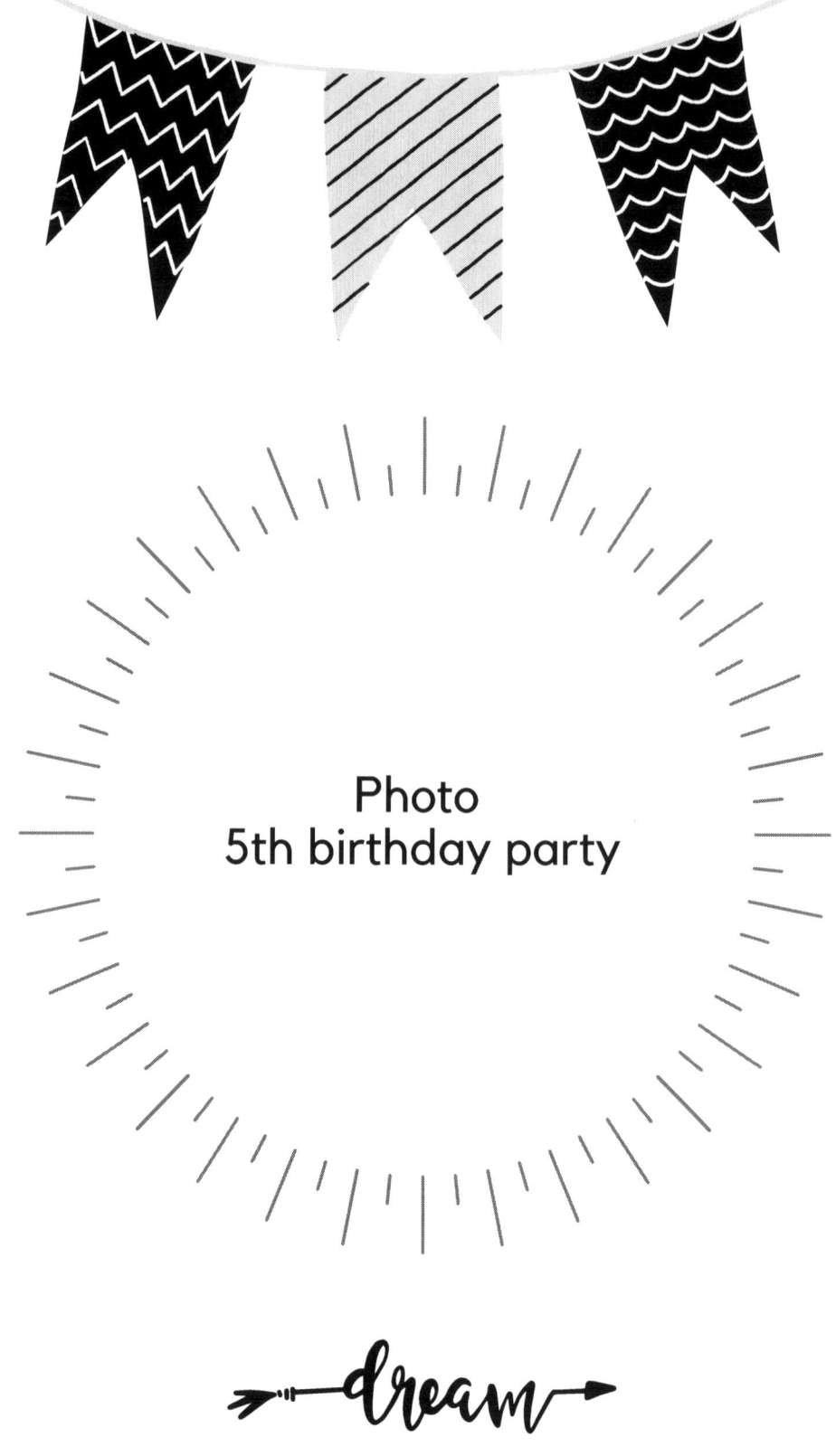

"You've been a blessing from the start.
I love you, son, with all my heart."

Date:

How we celebrated your 5th birthday:

What you're like at 5:

Best memories from this year:

My wishes for you:

My advice for you:

More thoughts...

Happy
Birthday

"You've been a blessing from the start.
I love you, son, with all my heart."

Date:

How we celebrated your 6th birthday:

What you're like at 6:

Best memories from this year:

My wishes for you:

My advice for you:

More thoughts...

Happy
Birthday

7

Photo
7th birthday party

→ believe →

"You are my SONshine!"

Date:

How we celebrated your 7th birthday:

What you're like at 7:

Best memories from this year:

My wishes for you:

My advice for you:

More thoughts...

My wishes for you:

My advice for you:

More thoughts...

Happy
Birthday

8

Photo
8th birthday party

love

"Always remember you are braver than you believe, stronger than you seem, smarter than you think, and loved more than you know."

Date:

How we celebrated your 8th birthday:

What you're like at 8:

Best memories from this year:

My wishes for you:

My advice for you:

More thoughts...

Happy Birthday

9

Photo
9th birthday party

dream

"Sometimes, when I need a miracle, I look into my son's eyes and realize I've created one."

Date:

How we celebrated your 9th birthday:

What you're like at 9:

Best memories from this year:

My wishes for you:

My advice for you:

More thoughts...

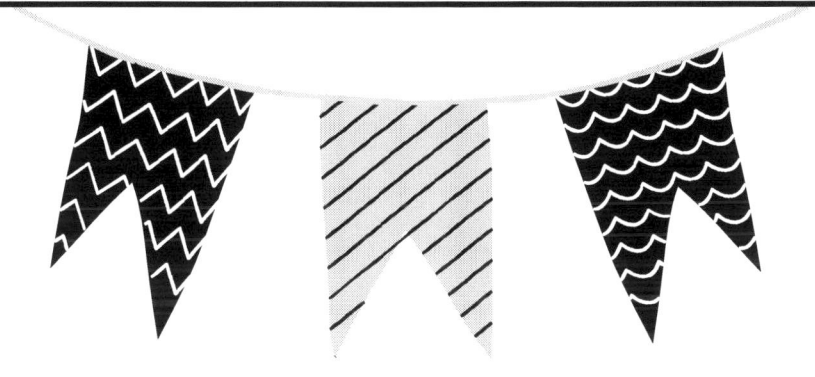

Happy
Birthday

10

Photo
10th birthday party

hope

"I may not be the best parent, but I must say you have proved to be the best son in the world!"

Date:

How we celebrated your 10th birthday:

What you're like at 10:

Best memories from this year:

My wishes for you:

My advice for you:

More thoughts...

Happy
Birthday

Photo
11th birthday party

believe

"Son, you will outgrow my lap but never my heart."

Date:

How we celebrated your 11th birthday:

What you're like at 11:

Best memories from this year:

My wishes for you:

My advice for you:

More thoughts...

Happy Birthday

12

Photo
12th birthday party

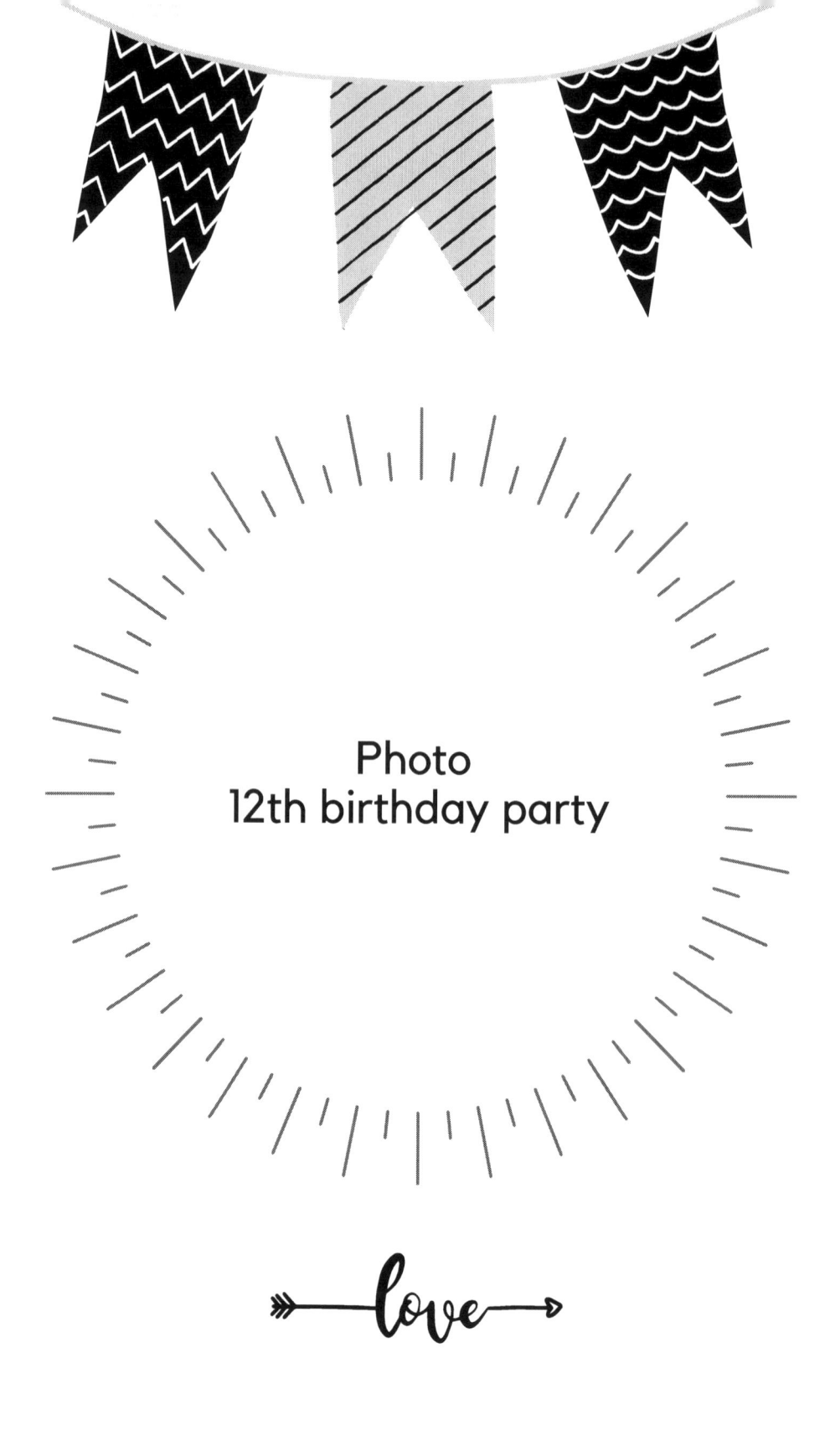

love

"My little boy yesterday,
my friend today, my son forever."

Date:

How we celebrated your 12th birthday:

What you're like at 12:

Best memories from this year:

My wishes for you:

My advice for you:

More thoughts...

Happy Birthday

13

Photo
13th birthday party

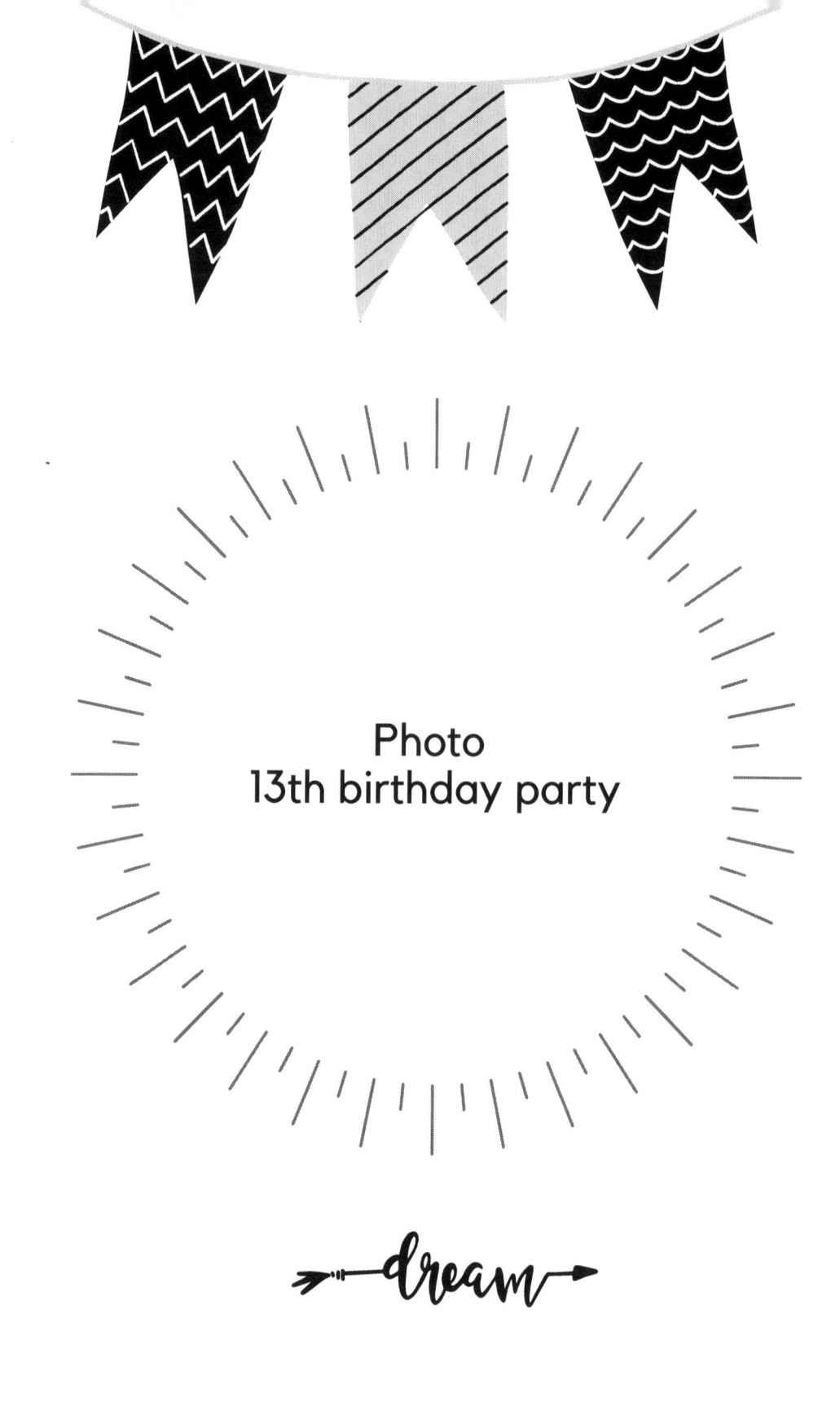

dream

"My wild, amazing son...run free! You'll know it when you're where you're supposed to be."

Date:

How we celebrated your 13th birthday:

What you're like at 13:

Best memories from this year:

My wishes for you:

My advice for you:

More thoughts...

Happy Birthday

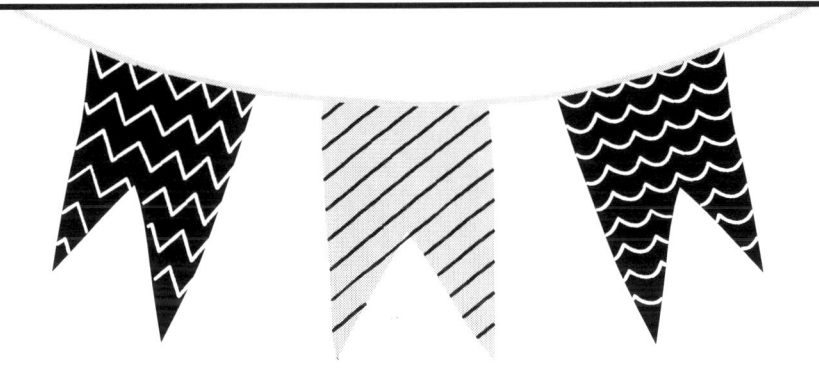

14

Photo
14th birthday party

hope

"I wouldn't change you for the world, but I would change the world for you."

Date:

How we celebrated your 14th birthday:

What you're like at 14:

Best memories from this year:

My wishes for you:

My advice for you:

More thoughts...

Happy Birthday

15

Photo
15th birthday party

→ believe →

"I will always be your number one supporter, for I care for you the most in this life of ours."

Date:

How we celebrated your 15th birthday:

What you're like at 15:

Best memories from this year:

My wishes for you:

My advice for you:

More thoughts...

Happy Birthday

16

Photo
16th birthday party

love

"Never forget that I love you. Life is filled with hard times and good times. Learn from everything you can. Be the man I know you can be."

Date:

How we celebrated your 16th birthday:

What you're like at 16:

Best memories from this year:

My wishes for you:

My advice for you:

More thoughts...

Happy Birthday

17

Photo
17th birthday party

dream

"I don't want you to follow in my footsteps. I want you to walk the path beside me and go even further than I could have ever dreamed."

Date:

How we celebrated your 17th birthday:

What you're like at 17:

Best memories from this year:

My wishes for you:

My advice for you:

More thoughts...

Happy Birthday

18

Photo
18th birthday party

hope

"There are two gifts I would like to give you: one is Roots, the other is Wings."

Date:

How we celebrated your 18th birthday:

What you're like at 18:

Best memories from this year:

My wishes for you:

My advice for you:

More thoughts...

Thank you!

We hope this little journal will be the perfect place to jot down a letter to your son each year, as you watch him grow. Include details about his childhood birthdays, your best wishes and advice for him, the way you see him in every stage of his journey towards adulthood, and any other thoughts you want to remember as the years pass by.

This will be one of the most precious gifts for your son on his 18th anniversary.

As a small family company, we'd appreciate your feedback on this book. If you like our journal, please send us your thoughts at:

sofiealexanderbooks@gmail.com

Love, Sofie ♥

Copyright 2022 - ALL Rights Reserved.

You may not reproduce, duplicate or send the contents of this book without direct written permission from the author. You cannot hereby despite any circumstance blame the publisher or hold him or her to legal responsibility for any reparation, compensations, or monetary forfeiture owing to the information included herein, either in a direct or an indirect way.

Legal Notice: This book has copyright protection. You can use the book for personal purpose. You should not sell, use, alter, distribute, quote, take excerpts or paraphrase in part or whole the material contained in this book without obtaining the permission of the author first.

Disclaimer Notice: You must take note that the information in this document is for casual reading and entertainment purposes only. We have made every attempt to provide accurate, up to date and reliable information. We do not express or imply guarantees of any kind. The persons who read admit that the writer is not occupied in giving legal, financial, medical or other advice. We put this book content by sourcing various places.

Please consult a licensed professional before you try any techniques shown in this book. By going through this document, the book lover comes to an agreement that under no situation is the author accountable for any forfeiture, direct or indirect, which they may incur because of the use of material contained in this document, including, but not limited to, - errors, omissions, or inaccuracies.